Money Management

Become a Master in a Short Time on How to Create a Budget, Save Your Money and Get Out of Debt while Building your Financial Freedom

Volume 1

By

Income Mastery

competence. There are no scenarios in which the publisher or author of this book can be held responsible for any difficulties or damages that may occur to them after making the information presented here.

In addition, the information on the following pages is intended for informational purposes only and should therefore be regarded as universal. As befits its nature, it is presented without warranty with respect to its prolonged validity or provisional quality. The trademarks mentioned are made without written consent and can in no way be considered as sponsorship of the same.

Table of Contents

INTRODUCTION

As you can see, it's all about the administrative fundamentals you have to take into account, such as your production, what you really produce, and what your offer is, or rather... What are you going to bid? After that, who's going to be the demanding public of your offer? I mean, who's going to need your product?

It seems long and tedious, but as you can see, it is a well-structured and defined planning process which will allow you to determine how much you need to invest and how much you can expect to earn in a period of time that you will establish according to the process of your production and the supply side of the market.

Remember that budgets can be public or private, and each budget is conditioned by clear and precise goals in a given time. Let's use a clear example: suppose you want to go on a trip with a family member or friend to a place close to your country or region. In principle, you will already be, in a decisive way, establishing the main objective: to go on a trip to a place in your country or region. This makes it a feasible goal, as you will be within your budget, if you are working and earning an income that will allow you to make that trip. Next, you will need to prioritize the steps to achieve that objective or goal. This involves following carefully some specific rules for achieving your goal which, as part of a plan, makes you commit yourself to fulfill it adequately because, in the end, you expect to achieve a positive result. Therefore, you will also have the participation of that person who will accompany you, and given certain steps you will include what actions the other person must perform to be part of your planned strategy in the time you want to achieve it. Once you have completed the steps and procedures to achieve your objective, you will have to make a decision which will be preponderant to delimit its scope.

Budgets, like most planned processes, are generally flexible and subject to modifications and unforeseen situations. That's why taking the above example, you may have realized that you still need to complete some fees to cover expenses necessary for your trip, or that suddenly you have exceeded your savings expectations and you have something left for buying some souvenirs or products that you want alternately to include in your trip.

With the example of the trip, we have touched on two other important terms: income and expenses or expenditures. To define an income, we can visualize an employee who offers services in a company; the payment he receives for these services is what is called income. This employee can receive income from other sources, such as tips, commissions, percentages or bonuses for production. This additional income will motivate the employee to improve and expand their production in such a way that they will look for tools with which they can achieve that goal. As you will see, this budgetary process is very much linked to our lives, and therefore it depends on our judgment to make the right decisions and stay in the production market; in the previous case, offering a service.

It may sound fortuitous to you that a particular person can earn an additional income, but, in fact, it is not; what happens is that when a person is in situations of self-demanding, he forced himself, in an "unconscious" and sometimes "intentional" way, to make and offer alternatives for overcoming and achieving a greater scope of net profits for his subsistence. Subsistence is understood as those means that are necessary to support oneself, in this case economically speaking. However, it must be clarified that subsistence also depends on planning and not only on improvisation, since it will never be linked as something fortuitous or improvised. Human beings tend to have instantaneous thoughts, which flow just like words in micro-thousandths of a second; in this process we let productive ideas flow into our minds and take them to action in a time we consider relevant. We can take this analogy in the same way for the budget, because when we clearly establish our goals and actions to follow, we define how we are going to achieve it, so as to then check our results with what we have planned; this way we are be able to improve our budget plan, as what we seek is to always have a positive balance and never expect a negative result because it would make us feel disappointed and discouraged, and always having as the final goal what we want to achieve in a determined period of time.

What are the differences between the budget of a private company and a public organization or institution? At first glance, the answer to this question seems easy, but one of the key points of the answer are incomes and expenses or expenditure, as mentioned in a previous example. Public institutions as well as private companies seek to meet goals or objectives but with a clear differentiation: they are subject to a cost plan and therefore, they are linked to a resource much more important than material goods, and it's is about human and qualified personnel. Without this resource, organizations and institutions would be unable to function properly and would not be successful in achieving their objectives.

If a food street vendor did not take into account the occurrence of plaintiffs in a place where he wanted to bid and offer his product, it would obviously be very difficult to achieve his sales targets, and that would lead to an inevitable failure and consequently, to a loss that will be reflected in his income.

The human factor as a resource is important to establish the action limit of the plans proposed for the achievement of the goals.

Another point to take into account is to determine how much responsibility will rely on the members of an organization to achieve the final goals. If you and your team are not clear about what you need to achieve, why you need to achieve it, and how you are going to do so, you will surely be creating an unstable environment for the direction and control of the actions stated from the beginning.

Let us then begin to prepare in a practical way how to elaborate a budget and improve our finances in our daily lives.

Chapter 1: Determine your income and expenses

How much income do you generate per month? It is usually a very difficult question to answer, but if you dare to determine it, you must also define how much net gain you will be able to obtain after that time. Once the answer to the first question is achieved, you can then calculate how much allocate to the expenses that we will be dealing with in the next section. To accurately determine your income, you must write down in an orderly and organized manner the money you earn for your effort and the time required to earn it. Your work is worth, as long as it is delimited in a space of time that will give the definitive characteristic to this work.

Begin with the income of greatest benefit, i.e. those whose value is greater within the indicated study time (a month); then continue with those of lesser value, taking the first one as reference. Once elaborated this classification, it is recommended to make a summation throughout the whole month taken a delimiting period of time for our record of income, to what we will denominate: monthly income record or income record of X month.

It is important to emphasize the accessibility to your income; even if you do not believe it, most of the income, as well as payments, that can be taken place in a store or trade, can be given in different ways: bank deposit, cash in current currency, checks, and the like. These different ways of receiving payment for your work make that, in a way, the income does not seem "real". If you pay attention to this, when you receive a bank deposit, it may be subject to the bank charging commissions, which causes your income smaller little by little. It is not intended or meant to imply that banks are bad for your income; on the contrary, they are usually a good way to plan your financial life and establish better economic projects. The purpose of this information is to determine the reality of the income received, so let's take an example: suppose you receive a job payment in a different currency from the official one; obviously, by changing it to your local currency, you will have a price that, in the end, will determine what payment has actually been received. This is true for people who, when they charge a service in foreign currencies, have an expectation of the cost of their currency, and are therefore conditioned by the movement of the supply and demand of prices of that currency.

Consequently, many people who receive an income in foreign currency risk that the price of that currency will be favorable when changing to their local currency, hoping to receive a higher income. Obviously, this is not a very common case in those countries where there are regulations for the entry of foreign currency.

Now that you can determine what your income is, then we can determine the expenses, which are going to be as important as the income; in fact, without them, we won't know what our real and exact net benefits are.

Expenses are as complex as our emotions and needs, so we must have greater accuracy for the recording and description of such information. Fundamentally, according to the administrative texts commonly used in universities, expenditures or expenses should be established based on a scale of categories of priority and importance. In this way, we have expenses that are a priority, that is to say, that we must obligatorily pay them, or else it will be much more difficult for us to carry out our goals in the determined period of time, and other types of expenses which, although they are not so necessary, usually are included in the set of expenses that derive from the priority ones.

Consider as a priority expense the basic home support services: electricity, water, telephone, gas, food, housing loan, rent/ room rent, apartment or house. While the non-priority, which we could call secondary, can be transportation, clothing, shoes, payment of commissions or external work such as repairs, cell phone plans, tv, internet, meals outside home and others. Of these last types of expenses come a smaller and feared group, since it causes a decrease in the personal income; they are known as "ant expenses", and they must be carefully examined. To avoid them is an obligation for any person who needs to improve and to precise effectively their income register. These expenses represent 15% of our total expense and, when added together, generate losses that affect our ability to save and invest. An example of this is those expenses that are made out of "whim" or caprice in situations or moments in which they are not essential, and they only generate superficial pleasure and satisfaction; this is the case of paying for a taxi when, in reality, you can resort to cheaper services, outing to the cinema just for the satisfaction and pleasure of seeing the latest movie premiere, the payment of commissions for late card payments, basic services and others. And so, there is another series of expenses of the same type that damage our initiative and monetary utility.

Once we have written down our expenses in a decisive way, it is important to make the sum of those expenses by ordering them from greater to lesser. In the description of each expense, we must take into account the period of its recurrence: that is, if it monthly, weekly, and the like. If we have more expenditures than revenues, we should not be discouraged, because that is when we must take action through a strategic plan to eliminate unnecessary expenses and increase the capacity to produce higher revenues.

The above lists can be compiled using summary or spreadsheets such as those of office programs and writing down as much accurate information as possible to make decisions that will help improve the situation we have determined. It is possible that all this information will serve us as a study for our financial development strategy, and will make us think well when it comes to spending the money that we have earned arduously and with much sacrifice.

Another recommendation when writing down expenses is to classify them according to their need, for example household expenses, personal expenses, food, etc.

Chapter 2: Deciding and using a control tool.

After writing down your expenses and income, it is time to determine exactly what or which control tool will be necessary to reduce expenses and increase income. Make a simple calculation to know what our net profit is; if the profit is positive, we will have a surplus, if it is negative, there will be a deficit.

If we have a surplus, the strategy to use will depend on our needs. For some people, the best option would be to invest the profit obtained from the subtraction of expenditures; for others, it would be simply to follow a saving plan to acquire a necessary good.

A very common control tool is the shopping list; another it is a production or sales budget, if it is the case to increase revenue.

For others, the control of their budget is carried out by means of templates of updated records of data of expenditure and income. Regardless of the chosen tool, the purpose will always be to control both the expense and income generated in the time required for that purpose.

Once again, when determining whether there is more expenditure than income, the first thing to do is to start reducing those of high incidence that drastically decrease your income. There are expenses that are fixed and you cannot do without them; however, we could look for alternatives that reduce their output, as for example buy cheaper or on sale products, travel in a cheaper means of transport, avoid the excessive use of basic services at home, such as telephone, electricity, water and others. There are other expenses called "ant expenses" whose impact on the budget are very catastrophic and harm the personal and family welfare, this is the case of dining out or buying in restaurants or cafes. The best control tools for recording expenses and revenues are data collection templates combined with written or date-printed expenses backup, incurred in a weekly or monthly period.

To use or apply these templates you need sophisticated applications such as spreadsheets; office software tools are very useful for these cases, given their versatility from a computational approach. Also, a database record could be used, as well as saved receipts, ballots and consumption invoices. In the same way, databases connected with graphical applications could be developed so as to show graphs and summaries of all our expense and income distributed in a time determined by the system. There are other tools as simple as the previous ones, such as financial and accounting management software, which facilitate the registration task without specifying the required fields, as such software take what they need form the information provided by the user, and process it into reports and calculations that are then displayed on screen when needed and required by the operator.

Obviously, for those who do not trust electronic tools completely, they can continue using pencil and notebook, and there insert the necessary backups so as then project the register results to make decisions to improve the results obtained.

Many experts usually recommend visiting the bank to consult and obtain financial advice about your money, but this is worth when you have a base capital to manage your finances. However, there are people who often could give you, on their own initiative, free help to your interest in saving and having better results on your future income by giving advice applicable based on your own interests, such as new ways of earning an income through small investments, or even how to carry out a saving plan to obtain excellent results in the future.

Returning to the subject of software, we find good options both online and offline; keep always in mind the fact that many take into account the total income and expenditure to give a council or reference on your financial management. A very productive couple long ago wanted to know how it was possible that their income faded so quickly, when they could have had a very good and regular income throughout the year; they realized that after obtaining a certain income, they spent approximately 90% of what they had generated and therefore, there was no progress in their savings. This had very negative consequences, and thus much tension in their relationship. After applying registration techniques and detecting where their funds were going, they were able to take more decisive actions and also achieved a saving goal that grew more and more over time.

All these details could be verified through financial assistance and using a personal financial management software. They carefully reviewed each of their expenditures, and through the calculations made, they observed in detail what these excessive expenses were and what alternatives could be applied. Obviously, this is the importance of using technological tools, because when looking for a certain period of time, it is faster to obtain results, which allows you to make decisions that will help solve the problem. Clearly we know what our biggest problem is: our income disappears, but there are much more interesting problems in which researches will give us more light and reflections on how our income, in which we have put so much effort, is evaporating and how we can prevent it from leaking. That is why we must break down our greatest problem into smaller sub-problems that will allow us to define in an essential way the strategies to be followed to achieve our goal of having greater incomes than expenses in a set period.

It is not easy to have the eager to realize those financial mistakes that have been made for so long, and even trying to improve them, not many people manage to cut them down and change their way of thinking and acting regarding money. It is a challenge for all people, when the will and longing for improvement must prevail in order to sustain the triumph from beginning to end.

In this section, it is worth mentioning a tool described by Nóchez Bonilla on Gestiópolis website, where he defines a technique called the "The tree of income and expenditure", which aims to observe, through an appropriate analysis, economic inputs and outputs (income and expenditure) that negatively influence the budget of any person or social group to seek and implement strategies to increase income (inputs) and decrease expenditure or outputs. The most remarkable thing about this technique is the emphasis it makes on the awareness that people who apply this tool must have, and that they must be willing to change spending habits and apply new ways of earning income. Materially, what it seeks is to educate those who apply it even adapting environmental awareness actions and some other ecological trends, as well as it is expected to be applied in a group setting; this is because the more family members or acquaintances support us in the task of saving and budgeting, the easier it will be to have the eager to move forward and meet the final goal we have set. The following is a brief description of how this technique can be applied in real life and how much time we need for its application.

Initially, we establish a quiet working area with a relaxing atmosphere that stimulates creativity and harmony of thoughts. When several people participate in a session, it is recommended that each one places himself according to his comfort and freedom of development; then we look for recyclable materials to develop the activity, such as bottle caps, paper and cardboard reused or recovered from other elements, wood, pencils, pens and any other thing that serves to understand and register the activity.

At the time of drawing or sketching, the parts of the tree are presented in the following manner: roots, which will be the inputs, the stem, the person or persons from whom the income comes, and the branches represented by the outputs. The thickness and size of each section or part determines the importance of the income or expense, the coarser it is, the greater the importance will be. Once drawn the branches and roots of the tree, we proceed to observe carefully with critical mind both the roots and the branches to identify possible inconsistencies in each part, thinking about the design raised. Thereby, each person makes a call to himself to be aware of the arisen situation; and then, each one seeks to commit himself to a viable solution to strengthen those actions that will make him reach a feasible goal without losing time.

Finally, the participant makes a statistic and a graph of what was observed in order to carry out each of the required steps and writing down those considerations necessary to fulfill his project.

In the end, the purpose of using any of the tools mentioned above is simply to be able to control a personal or family budget; even that of a particular small business, due to its microeconomic structure of operation, is a well-set example for the application of budget control. From now on, it is only necessary to test and adapt each tool according to the needs and priorities established for each financial study.

To conclude, the importance of the tool used will always be to make you think about your ability to solve the expenditure-income problem. Since the greatest problem will always be represented by your expenses, it is necessary that you can pay attention and discover by your own those who have harmed you, and diminish them once and for all by establishing actions that will be carried out step by step to achieve the desired economic balance, with a view to developing and fulfilling yourself.

Chapter 3: In case of a deficit, use a strategy of income and expenditure reduction

Previously, we commented on the expenditure and income registration and control. Special emphasis was placed on expense, since it particularly affects income and causes very negative consequences in the environment of any person, institution or company. We will take into account the fact that being negatively affected by expenses, and duly analyzed by our records, we will employ some strategies that will make our income much more stable even with the possibility to invest in possible options for the future.

Once determined and committed to change your economic situation from deficit to surplus, then we will proceed to establish those actions that will make this a reality and in a determined time. Analyze each expense thoroughly, and establish a recurrence pattern of all of them; determine how necessary it is to use the money in each of them, and place them on a list of priorities; then look for alternatives that allow you to reduce or replace each of them with another that requires less money outflow.

You must begin determining which of your fixed expenses can be significantly reduced. If you really need extra money, you may consider working part-time, moving to a lower-rent apartment, getting a roommate, or renting a room of your home. There may be other saving ideas needed to make your goal a reality; there will always be alternatives for all those expenses that seem unavoidable. Suppose you want to save on electricity, you should become aware of where the most electricity is consumed in your home: it can be an electric stove, a microwave oven, a light bulb on for a long time, the use of high drain appliances which leads into an expensive consumption bill, and obviously you will have more to worry about if you don't take action at all. At first, you may find it difficult to get rid of some unnecessary services such as the Internet plan of your cell phone if you already have one included in your landline or cable television; the same can be done with water consumption, as well as those personal expenses that happen while we are fulfilling others, such as buying unnecessary things during market purchases.

If you still have trouble making ends meet, be sure to prioritize things like your mortgage or rent payment and car payments over unsecured debt, such as credit cards. The last thing you want is to lose your home or car. Not paying your credit card bills will damage your credit score, but it will also make your creditors more willing to negotiate an affordable payment plan with you. If you prefer, you can work with a nonprofit credit counseling agency to negotiate a debt repayment plan on your behalf.

The goal is to, eventually, pay off all the debt that is costing you more in interest than you could reasonably expect to earn by investing that money. For a conservative investor, it would be around 4% 6% for a moderate investor and 8% for someone more aggressive. If the interest rate is below that, it can be considered a good interest rate.

Once you know you can cover all of your expenses, be sure to pay yourself before you pay someone else, as you will automatically save some occasional expenses, such as vacations and holidays, as well as emergencies that may eventually arise. Ideally, you'll also want to do a retirement calculation to make sure you're saving enough for retirement, but for now, at least try to put enough into your employer's retirement plan to get the matching funds that are available to you. That's free money you don't want to leave on the table.

Now that your basic expenses and saving needs are covered, you know how much money you have to spend through no fault of your own on whatever you want, such as shopping, eating out and having fun. You and your spouse may have that amount in cash each month, but when the money runs out, it disappears until the next month. Anything you don't spend can be transferred. The key to conjugal happiness is that neither of you can question how the other spends his or her allotment.

After performing this exercise, our caller discovered that he and his wife could live within their means by simply eating less. They can also use their next bond and a small inheritance to pay off their credit card debt in 3 years. That will free up money they can use for other goals, such as saving for retirement and making some home arrangements.

The idea is to control your financial future. After all, you know how hard you work for your money.

Some people find it hard to motivate themselves to save, but it's often much easier if you set a goal.

Your first step is to have some emergency savings: money available if you have an emergency, such as a boiler collapse, or if you can't work for a while. Try to get a three-month spending on an easy-access or instant account. Don't worry if you can't save this right away, but keep it as a target to aim at. The best way to save money is to pay some money into a saving account each month. Once you have reserved your emergency fund, possible saving goals to consider may include:

- Buy a car without taking out a loan.

- Take a vacation without having to worry about bills when you return.

- Have some extra money to use while on maternity or paternity leave.

As your savings begin to grow, you can:

- Put more money in your pension. It's a great way to make sure you'll be able to live more comfortably later in life.

- Make an investment plan based on your goals and deadlines.

- Keep records of all your deposits and purchases. Record each in your check register, which the bank will provide to you.

- Print or download your monthly bank statement if you don't already receive one in the mail. If you are doing everything online, there is a software that can facilitate this step, and the budget.

- Do your own calculations of deposits and withdrawals to make sure your bank hasn't missed anything or lost your money. Reconcile line by line, making sure your checking register is the same as your statement.

- Find the final number on each monthly statement and work backwards; verify what has been deleted and what has not. Deposits that have not been settled must be subtracted from their balance. If your checks have not cleared, they should be added back to your balance until they are cleared.

Go line by line and keep in mind the rates you are charged. Seeing them up close may ask you to call and ask that some be removed, which banks will often do if it persists. Also, add any pennies of interest you have received.

Again, if you have access to a computer, or even a smartphone, this process can be automated using a software or financial application, saving you time and frustration. The goal is to review your cash flow, look for errors and learn from what you see.

After you've had the opportunity to control your income and expenses for a month or two, you'll be more aware of the areas that need to be adjusted. Maybe your initial monthly income estimates were off, or maybe you didn't take into account expenses like car repairs or veterinary bills. Make adjustments, but always balance inputs and outputs.

Once you solve all the problems in your budget, you must commit yourself to following it. However, there is no budget forever, so periodic reviews are the key to success.

If you get a promotion, for example, you can increase your discretionary spending and your saving goals. On the other hand, a layoff or fewer work hours could mean cutting back on spending until you restore your income.

Savings should be part of the plan. Financial planners recommend that your savings cover six months of income, enough to make up for a job loss or another emergency. You may find it helpful to open a separate saving account and gradually fund it until you reach your goal. Maintaining a separate account will make it more difficult to raid the emergency fund to cover non-essential items.

As mentioned, an emergency fund is crucial for your financial security. Start by saving 20 dollars per week. In a year, it would be 960 dollars, plus any interest for when the refrigerator stops working or when the transmission explodes.

Experts recommend looking at your tax withholding to find hidden cash. If you receive a large refund each year, you may need to change your marital status to receive additional money in your paycheck for an emergency fund, unless, that is, you are putting your tax return funds into that same fund.

Medical crises in particular can reverse a balanced budget. Negotiate large medical expenses, such as an emergency hospitalization, with the hospital. Almost every hospital negotiates rates. Often, if they are contacted immediately rather than waiting until the amount goes into collection, the hospital or the provider's office can set up a payment plan.

If not, a consolidation of medical bills can help, as it allows you to combine all your medical bills into one lower monthly bill through an agency or a bank loan. Not only does this make it easier for you, but the agreement protects your credit score because you can make payments on time. The disadvantage is that it may take you longer to pay off your debt in full.

Creating a budget is the first step, but keeping the budget is where you start to see real growth in yourself and more duration of your money. Complying with a budget can be a difficult task for people who are not accustomed to spending limits or self-discipline in their finances, so it is important to maintain a positive attitude toward the process.

Staying motivated can help alleviate some of the budget pressures. Consider it non-negotiable to set aside a portion of money month after month so you can expect a relaxing vacation at the end of the year. Finally, set realistic and achievable goals. Start slowly and develop a plan that works for you and your lifestyle.

You should always remember the importance of differentiating between what you want and what you need. You may not be able to get the things you want, but if you try, you'll get what you need.

How are wishes separated from needs? And why bother? For many of us, knowing where to draw the line can mean the difference between creating a successful budget and going bankrupt. So what's the difference? Most needs are synonymous with non-discretionary expenses. They include shelter, which requires payment of rent or a mortgage, and food, which results in grocery bills. There are many other items that are basic and non-negotiable, but the non-negotiable category leaves room for choice.

For example, if you need a car to get to work, you can buy a used vehicle or a new one. The price difference is huge, and a less expensive brand is sure to impress your friends and offer an excellent driving experience. The question is, what can you afford? If you make 50,000 a year, the used car could be yours without stretching your finances. But if you take home 4,000, it's better to keep the used one.

The same rule applies to housing: should you rent a one-bedroom apartment or buy a 40,000-square-foot house? Once again, both offer shelter, but at radically different costs.

There is also a difference between the needs and the elements by which you could live without them. Think about taking a vacation in Thailand instead of a week driving to state parks near your home. Both can offer satisfying and relaxing places to pass your center, but the costs are radically different. Also think about impulse buying. Let's say you go to the home repairs store to buy some lawn fertilizer, and then go back home with a lawn mower you hadn't planned to buy. You may need a new mover, but it's a good idea to research models and prices before reducing your money.

Knowing the difference between wants and needs is the key to a successful budget. You can budget for some impulse purchases or product upgrades, but understand what you're doing, show moderation, and always make sure your budget is balanced.

Chapter 4: Record template use and projected and stable future income management

Budgets are living documents. Just as life is constantly changing, so are the demands on your budget. For that reason, it's a good idea to regularly review your budget to adjust for changes in your income and expense.

What should you consider? On the income side, you must make adjustments if you get an increase or receive an unexpected gain as an inheritance. You must adjust if you lose your job or move to a new one. Getting married or divorced requires a massive reworking of your budget, just like having a child. Sometimes the changes are smaller or temporary, for example, a health insurance co-payment may require a temporary adjustment.

You don't need to revise your entire budget when changes occur. The rent is the rent, and it is unlikely that you will change what you spend each month on your car. But other things are more flexible. If your income falls, you could eat less. If it increases, you could save more, pay off the debt faster, or make a discretionary purchase.

There is no strict rule about when to revise your budget. Some financial consultants suggest doing it constantly; others suggest revising every few months. It's probably a good idea to consider reviewing your budget when life-changing events occur, and setting intervals to adjust for smaller things like inflation and changes in fixed costs.

You should consider making automatic savings as part of your budget. What is an automatic saving? It's the money you set aside to fund an emergency account, pay for Christmas gifts later in the year, or create a college fund for your children.

Automatic savings are best handled by retaining paychecks. If you are saving for retirement and your company offers you a plan, sign up and money will be withheld from your paycheck. Many employers also offer medical and child care saving plans, which are generally tax-exempt. You can also automatically deposit your paycheck into a checking account and then transfer part of the payment to a saving account you don't plan to touch.

There are many strategies for automatic saving. Talk to a financial advisor to learn more about your options and the amount of savings you can afford. Once you implement a plan, keep it. Percentages will vary, but if your company will match contributions to your plan, save at least the maximum amount that will match. Other savings will be largely determined by your income and expense. If you need to withhold 20% of your paycheck to cover rent, be sure to do so. Knowing how much money you need and saving for it will ensure you to cover your expenses and prepare for the future.

Financial experts have presented recommended spending percentages to help people budget for the first time. For example, it is suggested that you spend no more than 30% of your gross monthly income on housing, whether you are renting or owning.

Automobiles are the next largest expense for consumers and probably the greatest temptation to overspend. The best idea is to keep spending between 10% and 15% of your monthly income. Anything beyond that stretches you, especially if a financial emergency arises.

Student loans can be another variable in your monthly budget. There are several income-based payment plans that limit your payments to 10-15% of your income. It's a secure number, but it will often extend payments for a few years and end up costing you a small fortune in interest charges. Try to use 20% of your budget, especially if you don't have a car payment or if you split the rent with roommates.

Other suggested percentages for current expenses include utilities (10%), food (10-15%), and savings (10-15%).

You must commit yourself to staying within the budget until you see results or stability. The best way to do this is to create an annual plan that covers your fixed costs, such as car rental and payment, your seasonal costs, such as gifts and vacations, and your discretionary costs, such as eating out and buying clothes. Work all these things into a 12-month projection and follow it to the letter.

If you find flaws in the plan or if your cash flow changes, you can modify it. Otherwise, try to stick to it. Consider using a software or a budget application to help you. If you discipline yourself, you'll be surprised as debts are paid off, savings grow, and your needs are met.

A budget forecasting approach can include bottom-up, top-down, public-origin, zero-based methods, to name a few. The methodologies for each can be divided into qualitative and quantitative. Qualitative is marked by the judgment of the budget owner, while quantitative is based more mathematically. Consequently, both qualitative and quantitative forecasting methodologies have their respective strengths and weaknesses.

Bias can significantly affect the usefulness of budgeting techniques, so it is important to consider the political aspects of a method. Whether a seller's need is to "play with the system" to increase the likelihood of reaching the bond or senior management needs to achieve objectives to appease investors, bias will often stress the budgeting process.

Simple quantitative methods also have their weaknesses. With a recent customer of mine, during his budget, he was using the average monthly percentage growth of the previous year to forecast product sales. While this is a very reasonable approach, I pointed out that percentage growth fell during the year. The use of that full annual average could lead to a systematic aggressive prognosis if the trend continues or even stabilizes.

As a personal opinion, quantitative processes are the best option to combine with qualitative processes, since they help verify the error verification assumptions based on the previous problems. I recommend a quantitative basis, as it is quick and relatively unbiased. It also explores the company's "function-defining" relationships between expense and revenue, as well as growth trends. Such methods are also more useful for a scenario planning, and can be a good basis for benchmarking and ongoing forecasting.

Because everyone's financial situation is different, you may find that not all categories in spreadsheets are applicable to your income or expenses. You may even recognize that some months are different from others, but after some exercise you should find that you are more prepared for those changes and that you are also accounting for unforeseen expenses.

Although a monthly budget cycle is generally the most reasonable time to establish a personal or family budget, there are many sources of income and expenses that do not perfectly follow a month-to-month schedule.

In that case, calculate how that adds up to more than one month and write it in the appropriate row and column. You may also have certain expected or even recurring expenses that occur more or less frequently than monthly. To count those expenses (such as auto insurance) in your monthly budget, simply calculate the total expense for the calendar year and divide it by 12 to find the "monthly" expense. Write that number in the appropriate row and column.

To get started, gather all your relevant financial statements, such as your pay stubs, credit card bills and any other information that helps you make the best and most accurate estimate of your expected income and expense.

To begin your budget, fill out the monthly budget amount column in the "expense worksheet" as best as you can for the next month. If a certain category does not apply to you, you can simply leave it blank or enter a zero (0) in the box.

Over the course of the month, track your income and expense. At the end of the month, complete the "actual monthly amount" column and compare it to your original estimates. You may have overestimated the amount you would spend on clothing, but you underestimated the amount you would spend eating out. Write down the difference.

You do not need to do this exercise every month, but it is extremely useful at first, as it helps you develop the most accurate monthly budget for future references.

When it comes to money for short-term goals, financial experts say people should focus on saving rather than investing. The money needed in less than three years must be protected from market volatility.

"Short-term investment is where people make mistakes," says Oliver Lee, owner of the Strategic Planning Group in Lake Orion, Michigan. "They see the bright light that says 6 percent and they come in." However, those types of returns generally require people to take risks they shouldn't have with the money they'll need soon.

For short-term goals, try one of the following short-term investments:

> High yield savings accounts.

> Short-term bond funds.

> Fixed income funds.

> Structured notes and others.

People should forget investing the money they may need in less than a year. Instead, find a high yield saving account to keep the money safe and yet available as soon as you need to use it. The money in a saving account is insured, and therefore safe from loss. Money market accounts are another short-term investment option. "While the Fed is currently lowering its rates, there are many money market funds that provide a reasonable return on short-term cash," says Lockyer. They may offer a comparable interest to some others and come with fewer restrictions. However, you may only be allowed to make a limited number of withdrawals from your account each month.

Similarly, fixed income funds offer a relatively stable way to obtain a higher return than that offered through saving or money market accounts. Many of these funds include bonds, but they may also include other securities. Fixed income funds do not offer much in terms of returns, but they are designed to minimize risk and limit losses in a declining market so that they can make good short-term investments.

Michael Windle, a certified retirement income professional and owner of C. Curtis Financial in Plymouth, Michigan, says people sometimes make a mistake thinking they need to save thousands of dollars before they can invest in fixed income or other market funds. "Instead of depositing money in a saving account, just put it in [investments]," he says. Doing this can help them improve their overall performance.

To get money from the one you won't need for at least three years, consider placing at least a portion of it in stock markets. Since most bear markets last nine to 16 months, someone who invests with a five-year time horizon can afford the risk of a bear market. Your investments are likely to recover before cash is needed. However, to be safe, people should start transferring money to fixed income funds and bonds as it nears when it will be used for the intended purpose.

Mark Charnet, founder and CEO of the American Prosperity Group, a financial firm based in Pompton Plains, N.J., says workers should be aware of how much time they have to compensate for the losses they generate. They also need to move their money to more a conservative and less risky investments as they approach retirement.

You must take into account that, in order to improve your income or receipts, you must always assume savings as a method of forecasting in the event that a mandatory need arises. In this way, you will be protecting yourself from unforeseen expenses which will always arise in one way or another, by making imbalances in your income and therefore the budget set in your plan.

Conclusion

By clearly defining the concept of budget, its usefulness and its importance, we have also identified various types of budgets that can be applied according to the type of organization. The mentioned tools will be the key to guide a better theoretical-practical application in the administrative processes of any company or in a personal way. In such way, knowing the main concepts associated to the budgets will be very useful to elaborate predictions of your sales, resources, production, finances, time, optimization and any other activity associated with the normal cycle of your life or of your company.

Entrepreneurship begins precisely by evaluating our life, the actions that help us and those that harm us. Certainly, sometimes it is difficult to accept or identify what everyday things are damaging to us preventing our progress in the consolidation of our goals; it is there where effective decision-making will make the difference between moving forward or stopping. Things do not reach our hands in a magical way; it is necessary to start for our inner peace to ensure right and just decisions for ourselves and for others. Generally, when you earn an income, there is a dilemma between what you like and what you really need. In this sense, we must organize the equitable distribution between basic needs and a fund of money (savings) to cover unforeseen emergencies that may or may not arise today or in the future. Similarly, it is very important to keep a monthly amount of money in order to prepare for a future retirement.

Each day represents a new miracle of life and hope especially when it comes to responding to the dynamics of a society in constant growth; that is how challenges represent a reality to which we must adapt with a clear conviction of growing in the spiritual, familiar and, of course, in the financial field, since only in this way will we gain space for both growth and peace. When we are calm, we are productive in our work spaces, more successful when we are cautious in making really effective decisions and safer in our interpersonal relationships.

Expenses should not overwhelm us, as they can be organized to meet needs without falling into excessive debts that compromise year-end profits. In this way, we can balance the public services of our main home (water, electricity, telephone, gas, toilet, internet, residence, among others), we must also include food, health, transport, recreation, although the latter is not a necessity, because we can share a pleasant time with our family group generating an atmosphere of integration, and I did not mean that it must be an ostentatious expense that compromises the entire income, it can even be a meal at home different from the rest of the other days, an outing to the park or simply eating an ice cream; the important thing is to give a smile to our children, what will give us joy and encouragement in difficult times.

In addition, within our organization, we must not forget the routine health check-ups, which will greatly reduce costly treatments that affect us both psychologically and economically, because the dilemma becomes present again by addressing your health or the fundamental expenses of your family group. Now you must keep in mind that if you forget eating, resting, taking vitamins, and going to the doctor for routine check-ups, you will no longer be a point of support for your family, but a concern as you convalesce in bed. While it is true that some diseases appear and we can do little to prevent them, it is also true that a good state of mind and properly take care of ourselves will decrease the chances of a serious illness to be diagnosed in time, as the best gift for our loved ones is not the most expensive phone, but the warmth of a hug every day, a smile on arrival and a word of encouragement in their most difficult times. We are all very valuable to others, do not be just a memory for not taking care of your health in time.

It is necessary to have a balance between income and expense, so as not to overburden our true capacity to pay. When we realize our reality, we will be able to recognize if our decisions have been correct or, unfortunately, we have made unnecessary expenses. Recognizing the wrong decisions is the first step to allow a significant change in our lives, and make provisions that will allow us to cover expected as well unexpected expenses, which may appear at any time, and only with serenity can we succeed in such unforeseen situations. In the same way, saving is a valuable lesson that we must teach to our children from their first years of life and we begin to develop this by example.

There are expenses that can be cushioned in several months to avoid excessive expenses in a single month; in such a case we can rely on the use of credit cards, which allows us to cover expenses and pay progressively in an accessible amount to our monthly budget, which will allow us to generate a positive record in the eyes of the financial institution in which we have our bank accounts, since in case of requiring an extraordinary credit the secret is to maintain a good payment record, which will show that we can acquire new credits. To do this, we must be responsible at the time of cancellation without waiting for notifications, direct discount from our bank accounts and even less be classified as a delinquent customer.

When observing our payment commitments, we can organize them according to the cut-off date, so we will have to cancel some at the beginning of the month as a priority and others at the end of it; thus, demonstrating to the service provider that we have the ability to meet on the expected date the commitments acquired, avoiding concerns about forgotten expenses. For this, we reflect them on a sheet indicating the assets to the left and the liabilities to the right in order of importance.

An adequate standard of living should be a priority, since if we eat well, we can be productive and reduce the risk of disease. In this sense, it is also necessary to balance work, rest and family sharing, since it is useless to cover all economic needs if they do not meet the affective needs that are present in our day to day life. The complaints often reach such a point in which we cannot fall asleep, which affects our quality of life. The key words are serenity, wisdom and firmness. Serenity is the key when facing situations without despair; wisdom in making decisions and firmness in maintaining the changes that allow us to be happier and more productive. Save not only money but also time by performing simple, everyday tasks in the shortest possible time as this will lessen your worries and increase your peace of mind by demonstrating that the effort was rewarded with success.

This practical text has had as mission to make you understand and value the subject of the budget as part of the administrative processes within the planning, as an irreplaceable instrument to predict the course of the company based on assumptions that allow you to open the way to corporate and business success so that then you can improve your financial life and establish economic values for your development and advancement in the business world. In general, it seems that the budget represents mostly the expense that can or must be made to achieve an economic beneficial goal; remember that, before the rigidity of a budgetary plan, it is necessary to take into account the judgment the planner establishes to define the follow-up criterion on the organization goals.